Life in the Second Circle

Life
IN THE
Second Circle

POEMS BY

Michael Cantor

For Julie —
Thanks for being such
a good poetry-buddy!
Mic

ABLE MUSE PRESS

Copyright ©2012 Michael Cantor
First published in 2012 by

Able Muse Press

www.ablemusepress.com

Printed in the United States of America

Library of Congress Control Number: 2011945743

ISBN 978-0-9878705-5-1

Foreword copyright ©2012 by Deborah Warren

Cover image: *Brown Possession* by Fritz Scholder, © Estate of Fritz Scholder

Cover & book design by Alexander Pepple, Valori Herzlich

Able Muse Press is an imprint of *Able Muse:* A Review of Poetry, Prose & Art—at www.ablemuse.com

Able Muse Press
467 Saratoga Avenue #602
San Jose, CA 95129

for Valori

Acknowledgments

I am grateful to the editors of the following journals where many of these poems originally appeared, often in different versions or under different titles:

"Still Life," "Looking Back," *14 by 14;* "At the Crafts Museum at Asheville," "Variation on a Theme by Marc Chagall," *Angle;* "Two Love Stories," *Anti-;* "Japanese for Beginners: *Ronin*," *The Atlanta Review;* "Summer Island," *The Barefoot Muse;* "Solo," *The Buckeye Review;* "*Katachi*," *The Comstock Review;* "Two Tales from the East," "What Would the Wind Drive?" *The Cumberland Poetry Review;* "Encounter at the Hotel Moskva, 1989," "The Journalist," "Buying Sneakers," "Dinner at the Inn of the Anasazi," "Pretty *Gaijin* Boys Have Often Been Her Weakness," "Travel Memoir," *The Dark Horse;* "The Zealot Tries on a Burka," *The Eleventh Muse;* "The Man Who Painted Women," "Freshly Shaved and Barbered Well," "Hexagram," *The Flea;* "Crossing Brooklyn Bridge at Night," *The Formalist;* "The Young Men in Their Beauty," *Iambs & Trochees;* "Life in the Second Circle," *The Larcom Review;* "The Rabbi's Son," "Ceremonies," "Aubadergine," "The Book of Five Rings," *Lucid Rhythms;* "For Harry, Who Had Three Passports," *Margie;* "The Man Who Caught the Pass," "A Game of *Go*," "The Unidentified

Civilian Speaks," "The Pundit," (the last two Howard Nemerov Award finalists), *Measure;* "Her Latest Girlfriend Stole the Silk Tabriz and Left a Cat Behind," *Merrimack Poetry Review;* "Penelope Lunches With Friends," *Off the Coast;* "Jump-Cut," "Jane," "A Brighton Beach Princess Remembers the Past," "Christina's Fantasy," "Overheard at Park and Fifty-Third," "Retired, and Living in Seclusion Near Las Vegas, Khan Reflects," *The Raintown Review;* "Muhammad Ali Entered My Dream Just to Say Hello," "The Performer," "Box Men," "Sketches From Route 1," "Death Watch," *The Shit Creek Review;* "Because She Fell Out of Her Yoga Pose," *Snakeskin;* "Ceremonies," "Venetian Aubade," "Where are the Negligees of Anthony?" *Soundzine;* "For Trudy, in New York on Business," "The Book of Tea," *Texas Poetry Journal;* "In the District of the Translators," *Think;* "Watching Reruns," "Buster and Etta," *Tilt-a-Whirl;* "The Sugar Man," "Antwerp, 1961," "Prologue," *Umbrella.*

"There Was a Woman Once," "An Incident of Honor at Bar Manos in Akasaka," "In the Spring of 1978," and "The River Children Come of Age" originally appeared in the chapbook *The Performer* (Pudding House Publications).

I wish to extend my deep gratitude to the many friends and colleagues in the Powow River Poets of Newburyport, MA, and the *Eratosphere* online poetry site, with whom I have workshopped and traded advice and poems and opinions and gossip and recipes and whatever-else-was-possible for many years, for bringing me into their community of poets, and providing the support and encouragement that helped enable my writing and this book. I would like to list you all by name, but there are simply too many, and I don't want to overlook anybody. My thanks to all.

Foreword

MICHAEL CANTOR USES WORDS TO paint and sculpt the world. He writes the world too—which I don't say as an afterthought, since verbal wit is Cantor's forte. But I want to be sure to mention right up front the 3D nature of the Cantor universe. *Life in the Second Circle* is a sensory kaleidoscope where the poems are more like movies. In "Jump-Cut," the speaker says that *film absorbs a life;* you could say the same of Cantor's poetry. And, although another poem refers to *life being life, the bitch it wants to be,* life for this poet is irresistibly wonderful.

I'm going to quote liberally from Cantor's poems, but I'm not issuing a spoiler alert—for three reasons: Since his words *are* his work, I can't do justice to their peculiar charisma without dropping a few lines. Secondly, the poems offer dozens—hundreds—of delectable Michael Cantor phrases for you to discover. Third, I can't resist.

There are Cantor's women, for instance (to mention only one category), often with attributes not necessarily attractive: a *faint incipient mustache; loose and mottled flesh.* There's the wife, *short and squarely built, who chewed her lip*—the detail that brings her to life. My favorite, though, is the woman who has a *red mouth bursting with kisses.*

In fact, one of Cantor's specialties *is* women (and the relationships of the sexes). Check out the lament entitled "Her Latest Girlfriend Stole the Silk Tabriz and Left a Cat Behind." Or take Jane with her *errant gene.* Or take the man who spins himself romantic images about a woman at a café but who asks himself whether he's *only seeing what I'm seeking.*

Cantor's cinematic vividness makes him a supreme master of Zeitgeist, who captures time and place in jewels of verse-drama: a poem about the movie *Breathless* nails the *grainy black and white of Paris in the Sixties.* The largely-forgotten title character in "The Man Who Caught the Pass" becomes a *Rosencrantz, a Guildenstern, whose role was simply to be there.* The vintage terzanelle "Watching Reruns" provides another slice of life: *The weary talk, the crime scene tape, the crowd.* And it gets even better. About Genghis Khan, the title says it all: "Retired, and Living in Seclusion Near Las Vegas, Khan Reflects."

There's something in this book for everyone to relate to: the *latexed digit* of Dr. Brandon Wu, the ad for sneakers in Burberry plaid (*the look is wan, and jeune, and dégradé*), a T-shirt shouting ("FUCK MILK! GOT POT?").

As a photographer of the day and age, Cantor has a couple of other specialties. Cityscapes, for example. Of these a subset includes foreign, and sometimes exotic, locations. Cantor has worked in various countries; he can write from a resident's vantage point. There's "Antwerp, 1961" with its houses *shell-pocked* and its women's *bare, unshaven legs chapped flaming red.* He encapsulates Venice in a nutshell: *stone and the smell of stone.* There's a seamy scene, from Leningrad in 1989, with a pimp in an *improbable green leather vest* and a woman who, *fair hair, black roots, looked blue with fear*. There's another woman who turns into a sexual tigress when she's *a continent removed from Darien*—and that's only the beginning of the story in "Travel Memoir," a commentary on both the suburban couple and the narrator. Cantor's business career took him to Japan, which supplied goodly grist for the later poet's mill. Our legacy from his life there is several gleaming cameos of Japanese culture.

Not that he neglects his home country. On the contrary. We get the spectacular tackiness of Route 1 in Palm Beach. We visit the *Brighton Beach Princess* who exists in a space between boardwalk-and-Bingo and memories of Mother Russia. By the way, if I haven't said anything about Cantor as a formal poet, it's because with him a form never trumps the content: this poem requires seven rhymes on one sound, but given the subject matter, no one can accuse him of forced rhyme: *car, Czar, samovar, caviar, far*.

Cantor spends part of each year in Santa Fe. In one particular Southwest landscape we drive with him through *an ochre world where gods assemble stone on stone*, passing through *a plaza by De Chirico*—the poem is not a postcard but a big painterly panorama. Of course, Cantor is Cantor; so we also get *pancaked beer cans* and teenagers with *angry skin*.

Here's another poem whose title says it all: "For Harry, Who Had Three Passports." Most villanelles clunk along to their last repetend; but this one opens with *I knew a man, who had a man, who knew* . . . (and I'm not saying any more).

This Harry, by the way, styles himself as *a Jew without a tribe*. There's another, younger, Jewish protagonist featured in two poems: Jack Sugar, the Sugar Man, basketball player and rabbi's son. Cantor's great talent—what distinguishes him from other poets—is his colloquial edginess; but, most often, affection for his subjects glows through his mordant voice. The worldview of *Life in the Second Circle* is more philosophical than cynical: A sestina paints (I have to keep using that verb) an Orthodox *eruv* where mystics with their skull caps are surrounded by Hermès scarves, string bikinis and nipple rings, where—in a farrago of cell phones, joggers, drugs and gangsters—*half-mad sages link their arms to form a ring around the moon.*

Cantor wears his intellect lightly. He is not a Poet who takes himself Seriously; he's having too much fun. And he wears his tastes and opinions lightly, too. But his poetry is nonetheless serious business. Cantor—hip and retro-cool—flashes the world before us in Fifties Technicolor, neon, stereo, Imax, Sensurround. But he's not only a philosopher, he's also an urban/urbane romantic.

Of the poems in this collection, Cantor etches into my mind and memory three especially unforgettable pictures: "The Young Men in Their Beauty" melds worlds-apart settings into a gorgeous, fierce, and poignant montage of youth. Contrast this with a different image—the young Wind, leader of the pack, who rides a *big black, badass Hawg* before he fades into a tame and passive middle age. Finally, chillingly, join Cantor's travelers who wait in a chilling departure lounge not far from the obese man whose black clothes hide *rolls of moisture, odor and decay*, a companion we try to ignore but who haunts all of us in our travels.

—Deborah Warren

CONTENTS

III. Buying Sneakers

I.

The Young Men in Their Beauty

For Harry, Who Had Three Passports

I knew a man, who had a man, who knew
a man inside the Ministry. He said
his man was just the man to see you through

whatever difficulties might ensue
in sorting out the living from the dead.
I knew a man who knew a man. Who knew,

back then, what Harry really knew, or who
he'd ever helped, or who got screwed instead?
He was the kind of man who'd see you through

his pale blue eyes, and sense at once what you
most feared—and what you'd pay to ease your dread—
to meet a man who knew the man who knew.

I'm just a businessman, he'd say, *a Jew
without a tribe*—and raise his gleaming head—
but you can trust my man to see you through.

When others raged, he quietly withdrew,
and we all left, but Harry never fled:
he knew a man, who knew a man, who knew
the man who was the man to see you through.

The Man Who Painted Women

We watched you as you limned a woman's face
and body—got it right—the half-held breath,
the promise seen implicit in the eyes,
the tension of the shadows on her flesh,
and yet you seemed unpleased. You gave her pearls,
then scarves, to try to capture and reflect
an essence—stepped back further, further,
inserting dark green dabs to form a bed,
and built on that until you'd filled the space
with tables, bureaus, bottles, fresh cut flowers
lying in the fragments of a shattered vase—
a note, a spill of wine, a twisted mirror—
added windows and a door—and finally you
stepped out of one of them to freeze the view.

Box Men

for Joseph Cornell
Discretely gathered objects fill a box
in this ascetic world. No epic sprawls,
no *Guernica,* no sheets and slabs of paint
with messages of passion, love or hate.
Stuffed parrots, wooden balls, an antique spoon,
beads, gems, dolls, rings, an eyeball on a shelf.
Pasted paper etchings, pentagrams.
Coins, goblets, corks in bottles blue as sky,
penny arcade toys, a butterfly.
A woman in a frame within a frame
stares out at you, the visitor. Voices fall.
Shadow boxes fill a shadowed room
and, each by each, invest a paradox.
To think outside the box, become the box.

for Kobo Abé
To think outside the box, prepare a box.
Find one of heavy, corrugated board,
three feet square, perhaps, and four feet deep

(a standard size lends anonymity.)
Obtain a knife, some vinyl for the window—
duct tape makes the waterproofing simple—
use padding on your head to ease the load,
and hang your things inside on wire hooks—
a cup, a flashlight, thermos, extra clothes.
Practice first at home, and then take walks,
and notice how you vanish in a crowd.
They pass you by, you are unseeable,
and soon you'll have no need for doors or locks:
a Box Man quickly can become the box.

   for Sam Walton
A Box Man quickly can erect a box
once permits are obtained, the town convinced,
the access roads and services in place.
High walls, good light, an open indoor space:
the trick is not in how you build the things—
by now the crews construct them in their sleep,
slap on a row of jumbo shipping docks,
and move in goods and shelves within a week—
but how you visualize and run your business,
what you do with wages, costs and prices,
that lets the buying public see you are
far better, on the whole, than ma and pa;
until there's nothing left but parking lots,
and empty streets and stores outside the box.

6

for Muhammad Ali
No empty seats are scored outside the box
of ring ropes, canvas square and brilliant kliegs
that form a cube of light and heat and sweat
and smoke, and aftershave and whore's perfume.
And here The Greatest comes to show the world
the savage splendor of his youth and grace,
his rapid hands, the latest thrumming dance;
he gives a course on how to launch attacks,
and know just why and when to go to war.
The entourage no longer serenades,
but fans recall, and that part never fades:
Float like a butterfly, sting like a bee.
Head full of passion, mouth full of rocks.
What was inside is now outside the box.

for M. C. Escher
What was inside is now outside the box
of tricks where mathematics schemes and plots
with art in endless flights of endless flights
of stairs that end up where all arts have crafts.
Woodcuts, mezzotints and lithographs:
birds turn into fish turn into birds.
Here outside-in is inside-out as hands
and pens emerge to draw opposing hands.
Birds absurdly mesh with other birds.
Woodcuts, mezzotints and lithographs

show stairs that lead to where all tricks and crafts
apply to endless flights of endless flights
of planar mathematics, schemes and plots.
What was outside is now inside the box.

for le Comte Edmond de Grisy
What was outside is back inside the box.
A cloak is waved, a burst of smoke and sparks;
the girl whose body we've seen slashed apart,
her blood and entrails spattered on a screen—
then disappeared—has reappeared, intact.
A tiger reexplores its cage, a vase
returns, a coach-and-horses rolls again,
their magic done, the vanished all restored.
The box was stripped and emptied—six bare sides
displayed and thrust before the audience,
and yet a sly illusionist's deception
has somehow found a way to resurrect
them all, plus roses, doves, and cuckoo clocks.
Discreetly gathered objects fill the box.

The Young Men in Their Beauty

> There by the walls of Ilium
> the young men in their beauty keep
> graves deep in the alien soil
> they hated and they conquered.
> — Aeschylus, *Oresteia* (tr. Richmond Lattimore)

The perfect children play lacrosse on beaten fields:
resplendent, gold on green; one flourishes the ball—
net-slung, dead white—as if to rally swords and shields
to heed an ancient call to arms and give their all

> *against a scheming foe. But, see, the group that masses*
> *on a farther hill is tall, long-muscled, darker;*
> *defiantly the Iroquois make darting passes,*
> *hooting, clubbing; ash on flesh and gravel starker*

than a referee's whistle. The favored children swarm
across an April carpet, sprinting, sticks on high;
the young men in their beauty revel, safe from harm,
and fill the sun-struck day with cries that amplify

> *and echo between Mayan walls. Rude shadows cling to*
> *Chichen Itza courts as bone and skin meet skin*
> *and blood stains stone. A ball invades a chiseled ring*
> *set on a wall; and now the end-game shall begin*

to play on beaten fields: a bowl of hammered gold,
a hard black knife, the children perfect, bright and bold.

9

Jump-Cut

At the end of *Breathless*, when he dies—
Belmondo dies, that is, not Richard Gere,
in Paris, not Las Vegas; the original
and not the stupid remake—when he dies,
this handsome thug—Jean Seberg wipes a thumb
across her lips, the signature adopted,
message sent; her lover sprawled on cobblestones.
An angel blinks, and turns, and fades to FIN.

There is an ancient story from Japan:
a conquered feudal lord about to die
called blood and curses down upon his captors,
vowing that he would come back from death
to bring an awful vengeance to their lives—
burn lands and houses, savage wombs, kill all
the *daimyo's* men who viewed his headless body.

To be a jump-cut, loosely muscled hood
adrift in grainy black and white in Paris
in the Sixties—Christ, that was the dream
of dreams—a cigarette rolled lewdly in the mouth,
the frantic puffs, loose shirt, loose tie, a hectic,
jerky kind of motion that propelled us
in and out of bars and beds and automobiles
and down gray streets of tracking shots and death.

I have no fear of ghosts, the *daimyo* said.
One swordsman's stroke will end your life—at once—

and there it stops. But if you think you can return
to haunt and torture us, then send a sign.
Do you see this golden pennant with my crest?
If will alone can make your severed head roll on
this far, to grip the staff and hold it in its teeth—
it means you are a man who keeps his word.

Since Paris is the place one goes to dream,
Michel Poiccard/Belmondo joined my troupe,
and wandered with us down the Boulevards,
full-lipped and feline, arrogance and grace
behind dark shades. He played supporting roles
as well, in scenes set at Les Deux Magots,
and said his years spent on the run had taught
that film absorbs a life, and life a film,
and life evolves from cameras rolled on chairs.

The head fell straight, took one small bounce, and then—
eyes wide and staring, mouth agape, bumped on the length
of one man's arm, and when it reached the *daimyo's*
pennant, clamped its teeth down on the wooden staff.
A wind of ice went through the *daimyo's* force,
and then he spoke: *in order to become a ghost,*
to fight again, to seek revenge and blood,
a soul must think of nothing but that need
at the instant it finds death. He toed the head,
its eyes still open, teeth clenched fiercely on the pole.
This one thought only of its piece of wood.

Japanese for Beginners: *Ronin*

A *ronin* is a samurai without
a lord; a hired sword who boldly slaps
his sandals down the misted paths of sharp
Shikoku hills; and those he kills he knows

from their supporting roles in other blood-
soaked Kurosawa epic films: a priest,
a beggar monk, a warrior, a drunk—
one time he slew a *Daimyo* with one stroke,

fought bodyguards and courtiers—all slashed,
sent reeling, blind, through sun-bleached graveled courts,
to crash through *shoji* screens and flimsy walls
and die; their crimson handprints still alive

on swaying, spattered scrolls—then helped them up,
pulled out a smoke from deep kimono sleeves,
swept back his swords and joined the *Daimyo's* crew
at Toho's commissary buffet lunch:

a pleasant bunch—thieves, peasants, courtesans,
stout farmers, archers, artisans and such—
all *ronin* there, in service of the small,
age-beaten Lord in glasses and beret

who would quite soon complete his duel, his film,
his life—die too—the players left again
to slouch from inn to inn; to roam the land
without a lord, without a truth: *ronin.*

The Book of Five Rings

Musashi Miyamoto used two swords:
behind the long *katana* slashing blade,
the *wakizashi*—short—would almost fade
from sight and mind—then slide inside—and hordes
of samurai found misdirection kills;
their fighting cry became a blood-choked roar.
A master of the craft and art of war,
he sought the truths that lay beyond his skills.

And towards the end he switched to swords of wood,
withdrew into a cave, and drew and wrote,
worked at calligraphy, unwashed, remote;
he died alone and not well understood.

The Journalist

The *when* came first, and was no problem since
clocks hung on the market wall had stopped
precisely at the time he had to know,
and there were watches too, all smashed it seemed,
and parts of straps, and down the blackened street
a grand old tower timepiece still retained
an hour hand; and what was good was that
they all agreed: there was no fog or mystery.

W*here* was simple also, since the maps
and GPS coordinates all showed *this village*
or *that town*, and most had names, or he could
find someone to tell him *this is The-Street-
of-Music-Stores-That-Used-To-Be* or *here is
The-Place-of-Orange-Trees-That-Burned-All-Night.*
He would write it down slowly, in his way,
and soon began to find the names himself.

He often stumbled, though, at *what*, for *what*
was not so clear. *Some kind of IED,*
they'd say, perhaps behind a truck or car.
*Men came with masks and guns and called out names.
The belt is wrapped around a piece of corpse.
A woman, all in black, in line for food.*
He learned more acronyms, and all the vast
new nuances that came with *improvised.*

And next was *who*, and *who* turned out to be
impossible. The bloodstains on stone walls
were *who*, and headless bodies found in lakes,
and gunners torched inside their vehicles,
and chunks of flesh and fat; and still the questions
rang of *who was this and who did that,*
and *who* was shot or bombed beyond all moral
sense, and *who* was God to suffer this?

And when he came to *why* he took a walk
at noon, behind a berm of blasted earth,
and stripped off forty pounds of Kevlar vest
and shirtless, spinning, spinning in the sun,
leaned against a rock, and puked, and wept;
but still the sun remained, and still he went
on going out each day to sanctify
the old, old cry: *who, what, when, where, why?*

The Man Who Caught the Pass

This is the time of year, year after year,
in the rooms of this winter-dismal city,
when Billy Crowther, slim as a young god,
vanishes himself again and again
into an alien stadium's twilight, sees
that football arching, arching towards him
and somehow, falling backwards, reaches out
towards blackness, finds and grabs a golden ring,
and ends up on his ass, possessing now
a ball, a game, a life.

                  You can see it
as often as you want these days on YouTube—
twenty years ago, but always just the same
six seconds on the clock, the team down four,
as legendary Sweeney waves the crowd
to silence, sprints imperiously right
to find a quiet patch of turf, then plants—
and hurls—a sixty-seven yard long lightning bolt, a javelin
that Billy Crowther gathers in, becomes
The-Man-Who-Caught-the-Pass-That-Sweeney-Threw,
and that will be his name

                 forevermore.
Sweeney won the Heisman that next week.
It was The Play, they said, The Greatest Pass
That Ever Was. He posed and smiled handsomely,
turned pro, and was a superstar for years,

sold breakfast cereal, and pushed his charities.
Billy Crowther signed a lesser contract,
blew out his knee before the second game
and never played again—a cameo,
a Rosencrantz, a Guildenstern, whose role
was simply to be there.

                       His job was done.
We wonder what it must be like, at twenty-two,
to be so well defined, to spend your life
as anti-climax to an accident—
a safety gets confused, a coverage blown—
that's all it takes. The-Man-Who-Caught-the-Pass
is who you are, and almost every day,
unless you find yourself a mountain-top,
someone will bring it up, and you will smile,
and make a gracious joke, so they can think
how nice he is, The-Man

                     Who-Caught-the-Pass.
I met him once on business, recently—
a typical Vice President of Sales—
attentive, friendly, poised and capable;
and realized this was exactly what
he would have been if he had dropped the pass.
There was no tragedy to end the play:
he'd never spiraled downhill, never read
the script, was unaware how things should be.
Our business done, I called out as he left.
He paused, and turned his head.
                           "Nice catch," I said.

The Rabbi's Son

Jack Sugar slid away from Jacob Zuckerman
at *Shabbos* morning services; threw on a blue
and faded sleeveless tee, and grabbed a train downtown.

Inside the Fourth Street cage the black guys knew
that Jack was strong and fast; could make those tough,
quick moves and take it to the hoop and stuff—
but also had a point guard's street-smart sense.
So when he hit the court the whispers flew
about this uptown dude named Sugar, who
blew kisses to the *shiksas* near the fence,
then spun in mid-air, pumped a jumper, *dunked*

the winner as the great crowd's cheers drowned out the hum
of *Kaddish*, and he shushed them not to interrupt
the closing prayers, final blessing, and *"Shalom."*

The Sugar Man

At try-outs, sweet Jack Sugar was the one
with all the moves, who walked his sloping walk
as athletes do, who called himself The Hawk,
the Sugar Man!—who nonchalantly spun
two basketballs on fingers on a run
across the gym, and bowed as we all gawked.
But we were sharp, and mean, and soon the talk
was that he was all show—a greedy gun
who threw up brick on brick, and played no "D."
Jack had the *look* and style—smooth as glass—
but couldn't make a shot and wouldn't pass:
by next semester he was history.

Oh Sugar Jack, Jack Sugar, here's my plan.
You have to find a you that sets you free
to do just what you do—make style the key!
Be poet, politician, businessman;
you need a place where you can sky and soar,
and that's what counts—not baskets made or missed—
but misdirection, magic tricks, and twists;
and how you look is how they keep the score.

Freshly Shaved and Barbered Well

I arrive the town in my green tin truck
with wire wheels, and mermaid-colored sides,
and wave about a sapling dowsing stick
until the townsel lads and dumplings gather.
There then I flicker-flack my bumpled snout,
and thrust bouquets of seaweed at the crowd.
Fish, belly-up in the shallow inlets,
will swim and see again, I promise them,
For the dowser-man is here, and he knows
streams and rains, and all the secret ways
beneath the church and school; and with my smoke
and mirrors, images and rhythm spells,
and forked young rod and cymbals, pipes and drum,
I have such tricks as make the public hum.

Solo

At first, the dancer's steps are tentative—
a barefoot, *a capella* patter-pit
with squeaks on every pivot; delicate
beneath a floor-length cape that seems to give
no countenance to light: dead black and matte
it smothers all, a tomb. Diminutive
amid the grandeur of the room, the cape
and dancer bend to one another's shape.

A tambour stutters an initial beat,
and as its rat-a-tat intensifies
the dancer whirls—a slash of muscled thighs
across the stage—a leap, a quick retreat
into the gathered cape, a fall and rise.
Now bagpipes, drums and bugle calls repeat
the slapping of his feet: the music skirls
and soars, the dancer crosses left, unfurls

the cape—its lining shining, silken red!
And brings it huddled, closed—then folds it back
to Mars-God red again, and weaves to black.
Red streamers fall, the dancer bows his head,
accepts bouquets, blows kisses to his claque
within the audience, well groomed, well fed—
the dancer taller now, stands straight and proud—
his cape turned on itself to form a crimson shroud.

The Zealot Tries on a Burka

I like this cloistered shroud; the narrow view,
the slit and mesh which let in dappled light,
but also serve to block out that which might
not quite agree with me. Convenient, too,
for I can move my head quite readily
and thus adjust the outside world to fit
to mine. The air is sometimes fetid,
yes, fresh breezes cannot enter easily,

but, see, the fabric flows down to my feet,
completely cloaks whatever lies inside
so, if I wish to veil my eyes, I hide
all from all sight—including mine—complete
the circle, mind and body circumscribed,
tumescent in my righteousness and pride.

The Unidentified Civilian Speaks

It isn't easy finding work these days
but, God be praised, my dear, dead brother's friend
heard of this job, and thought to recommend
me, as he knows that I'm the type who stays
behind the screen. My work? They write the phrase,
I move my lips—and then we both pretend
I said what I just said. They claim the end
supports the means, and promise me a raise.

The enemy is losing ground today,
for now we take the fight to them, I say.
There is so much to do, for we take pride
in swift response to each attack—and then
my words of simple courage sing again.
Of course, I cannot be identified.

The Pundit

The shrug works well to indicate disdain,
perhaps approval: no one can construe
for certain what, in fact, is flowing through
that solemn mind, and none can ascertain
his preferences; and thus, aloof, urbane,
he rumbles in each frequent interview
on what just could—or could just not—ensue,
or who might seize the day, or might abstain.

The trick is in the way he's learned to pause,
importantly, then drop a weighty name.
Such *gravitas* is how one plays the game:
he drawls out *war*, or *underlying cause,*
aware that all he really has to do
is intimate that he knows more than you.

II.

Encounter at the Hotel Moskva

In the District of the Translators

At the gates of the District of the Translators,
around a crumbling statue of a woman with no name,
who was said to have understood languages
consisting only of clicks and whistles,
who was descended from the birds,
and who drowned herself in a well when unable
to replicate the nuances of the love songs found
in a crypt above the city
                              —at these gates—
crowds of foreign workers surround each scribe,
dictating letters to prospective employers,
or government offices, or last night's lovers,
and they are rarely satisfied. The subtleties
of their own languages, they complain, cannot be written
in this crude tongue of their adopted land;
the way the conjugation of a verb
defines one's state of mind does not exist,
there is no word for the smell of fresh grass,
or for nostalgia for a favorite food;
and here the months and numbers have no colors,
and communication has become a joyless task.

Beyond the gates, the buildings of the Diplomatic Section,
cinereous and bleak, are clustered
on a hilltop well above the District.
Few sounds are heard here, fewer faces seen,

and those that do appear seem overburdened
with the thrust of every word and phrase
that slides, adorned in blue, from hand to hand
and tongue to tongue, transliterated and debated,
divellicated, re-rewritten, pondered
to avoid the chance of stating something
that could, somehow, be read by someone
as commitment to complete commitment.
In phrases muffled by thick drapes, the experts praise
each other for their diligence, and reminisce
on how a misplaced comma once set off a war,
and the power of the semicolon.

But it is the noisy, crowded quarter
where Poets translate poets that draws most visitors.
It is an awful, thankless job, a voice
within a tavern sounds, *no matter what you do,*
you cannot satisfy the lot of them.
Supplicants and critics line the twisting streets
that often terminate abruptly at a wall;
at times, outsiders, smelling of straw and tea
from days and nights in third-class coaches,
appear with an entourage of friends and lawyers,
waving glosses and demanding an apology.
When you get it right, another drinker cries,
and all the hidden subtleties are there,
the metaphors all working as they should—
well then they tell you that it doesn't rhyme,
or it doesn't wind along the way it did,

or that the scheme has changed—and then that's fixed,
in a language with a dozen vowels—
and some fool says that you have lost the feeling
that is essential to the blah-blah-blah.

Among the Poets ranged in endless corridors,
life consists of weighing this and that
to find a middle path, of bartering
a deft allusion for a hard-edged phrase.
A fretful hum runs through the rooms,
for what devolves of compromise is that the Poets
are said to find an antidote in passion,
making love to strangers willfully; indeed with fury.
At dawn the cognoscenti fill the quarter.

Antwerp, 1961

There was a time when mornings were defined
by bicycles, and sturdy girls who rode them
to their office jobs through cold, damp, still dark
Flanders winter mornings: full of laughter,
as they lingered in the downstairs hall;
sweater sleeves pulled down to fingertips,
bare, unshaven legs chapped flaming red.

A time to pass the shell-pocked fronts of houses,
and see, and yet not see; look past the scars,
wash blood from clotted blood, put stone on stone,
restore the earth, rebuild and resurrect,
and do not ask whose blood, what earth, which God,
but hope that something had been learned in blood.
There was this time, one time, and then it passed.

Encounter at the Hotel Moskva, 1989

The way his hand appeared to commandeer
that ass, it seemed he had to be her pimp,
in an improbable green leather vest
in Leningrad, midday, mid-June.
And she, fair hair, black roots, looked blue with fear;
both legs were trembling as he moved to primp
her perm, tugged at a too-tight skirt, caressed
tensed hips and thighs while I looked on.

They whispered, then the hand pushed at her shoulder:
impelled, she crossed the street, slid past a brace
of pockmarked doormen, vanished in the entry,
and he was suddenly transformed—
rabbinical and solemn, pensive, older,
his hands behind his back—I watched him pace
the hotel's length: stout mentor, consort, sentry;
he waited, stolid yet concerned.

We shared the elevator, she and I,
much later in the day, an accident,
and recognized each other from the Square.
I nodded once, at once discreet,
observed a thin patch in her hair, the dry
scalp red and flaked; a soiled, acrid scent
rose from her blouse and lingered on the air.
Her eyes were focused on her hands.

The elevator trundled down, and we,
lone occupants, could hear each other's breath.
We did not smile, or speak, or otherwise
communicate. What could I have said?
And what was there that she could say to me?
Quote Gorbachev on *glasnost*? Note the death
of ossified old ways and compromise?
Discuss the Siege of Leningrad?

> *The city circled by a Nazi force*
> *nine-hundred days and nights, and somehow half*
> *survived: they lived on rotted fish, glue soup,*
> *and every spring the dandelions emerged*
> *and men began to weep. In forty-three*
> *a field of corpses rose through snow at dawn*
> *and charged the heavy German guns and won:*
> *this Russian madness is our secret weapon.*

She scuttled through the lobby, legs now bare,
returning to her stoic pimp's domain:
I followed, saw him locked in stiff reclusion,
preoccupied, big head turned down,
until he heard her footsteps; then a stare
of understanding, tenderness and pain
flicked on and off, and cut through all delusion.
In some mad way we shared her now.

Venetian Aubade

> And at the table next to me a woman,
> lobster-baked, a Campo veteran.
>   — from "Watching Women and Dogs on the
>   Campo S. Maria Mater Domini" by Rick Mullin

Another poet wrote of this *piazza*
and a woman there; and so I shamble
through a twisted city—*campo* and *terrazza*,
stone and smell of stone, streets that tumble
into dark canals—retrace and fumble
after someone else's view of Venice
and find her, terra-cotta, gold and umber,
streaked with blonde whose edge has lost its menace.
Her morning is a bare café and remnants
of a *grappa*, straight, and she is singing
to a cell phone, something mad and endless.
Or am I only seeing what I'm seeking?
This place of masks encourages disguise;
the soft Venetian air is where truth lies.

The Book of Tea

> The materials used in the tea-room's construction are
> intended to give the impression of refined poverty.
> — Okakura Kakuzo, *The Book of Tea*

Great care is necessary to deny
all carefulness; create a simple, spare,
and unobtrusive hut—
just four straw mats, an iron pot, some bowls—
which shapes its structured anti-symmetry
with twisted pines and water, stone and wood.
The Book of Tea demands the tea house be
imbued with understated poverty.

Katachi

Katachi: pattern
Wood grain in temple gateposts
Marks on a clay pot
Nests of lacquered food boxes
Crossed beams in a tea-room hut

> *Patterns fill a life*
> *Wood, paper, clay, stone, water*
> *Gestures, bows, words, looks*
> *Precisely follow studied*
> *Codes of ritual and style*

Overlapped roof tiles
Bundles of pine grave markers
Buckets and dippers
Woven straw *tatami* mats
Sandals at an entryway

> *There is a set phrase*
> *For meeting and for parting*
> *For begging pardon*
> *Expressing rage or sorrow*
> *For surprise, for love itself*

Country inn signboards
Pebbles raked in the courtyard

White powder, white neck
Noh masks of fixed emotion
Faces formed and carved with care

> *One must understand*
> *There is a way to wear clothes*
> *A way to drink tea*
> *Combine flowers, meet lovers*
> *A way to live and to die*

Flicker of a tongue
Over moist vermilion lips
Black ink and black brush
One scroll hanging, one flowered
Puckered silk kimono sash

> *Arranged relations*
> *One man, one woman, one life*
> *Without a question*
> *Patterns of behavior must*
> *Nestle like terraced rice fields*

Hands on a bare back
Flesh on shadowed somber flesh
Scar high on one flank
Moonlight strikes an inn's still pond
Carp flicker, silver and dark

As the earth's huge plates
Held together like roof tiles
Under constant stress
Sometimes buckle and break loose
Patterns can change instantly

Steaming cedar tub
Kiln-fired *saké* cups, damp curls
Hot-house sweet fragrance
Fresh, red, dew-spattered poppies
Forged steel blade, white wrists, black lines.

Katachi

An Incident of Honor at Bar Manos in Akasaka

Two beer bottles smash
Against a table, jagged
Edges carve at skin

Freeze frame at the bar
Then a face realizes
It was ripped, explodes

In blood *Fuck Fuck Fuck*
My eyes, he screams, and vomits
Some whores are crying

As the *yakuza*
Throw down money and file out
Bowing politely
In their dark gangster glasses
They whisper *Gomenasai*

Travel Memoir

"Foreign travel always turns her on,"
my colleague says, describing how his wife—
at home, "as straight and sweet as apple pie"—
loves to strip and pose and promenade
in strange new hotel rooms, the instant that
a door clicks shut behind a bellhop's back.
The clothes come off with swift and silent grace
blouse, bra, skirt, shoes, panty hose and panties
drop without the pretense of a tease.
Emboldened by their anonymity,
she bares herself to him and postures, preens;
    a continent removed from Darien.

We are deep in alcohol and leather,
this loose-lipped middle manager and I,
absorbing cigarettes and double scotches
all the way from Anchorage to Tokyo,
on a plane no longer flown, on an airline
long since gone, in a haze of memory.
Cushioned in our airtight cylinder
he rambles on; expounding on his spouse's
mons veneris and lavish pubic hair,
relating tales of games of sex in Bonn,
Madrid and Rome with husbandly delight.
The flirting ghosts of perfect, golden girls
    in powder blue refill our empty glasses.

In time, I had the chance to meet his wife,
at a business dinner, on the buffet line,
and over *coq au vin* and Brussels sprouts
I checked her out. I wish she'd reeked of lust,
and that a musky heat rose from her body,
and our hips grazed, then pressed deliberately
against each other; but that was fantasy.
Instead, I saw a pleasant, quiet woman,
short and squarely built, who bit her lip,
and had a faint, incipient mustache—
Frida Kahlo, less the burning eyes.
But the mind retains initial images,
and years later, hearing he had died,
the only picture I could recollect
was how his wife would settle, ripe and naked,
in a hotel chair, and start to touch herself;
    luxuriating in her cuntliness.

Expectations play their games with us;
memories will have the final word.
Although this happened forty years ago,
a silver tube still crosses the Pacific,
each perky stewardess still young and blonde.
The handsome captain strolls the aisle and nods,
and two inebriated passengers
    distract each other on a lengthy flight.

Ceremonies

I

I saw the Brazilian Olympic team strut and sashay into Meiji Stadium
      Tokyo, 1964, opening ceremony.
My friend Klaus in the outside row,
two years running, world champion, Flying Dutchman class,
here as the favorite with a brand-new fast new boat,
windmilled both arms over his head,
threw kisses to the crowd,
sang the anthem aloud like a big rube.
Stumbling to a samba beat,
he pawed at his eyes with huge sailor's hands.

I am the most Brazilian on the team.
It was me who decided to be a Brazilian.
I sailed twice around the world, and when I came here
I ate prawns cooked with lemon juice and coconut milk
in a straw hut on Praia do Salvador;
I watched the brown and gold girls on the white beaches,
and saw the mountains touch the sea.
I heard the laughter,
and the music.
When I came here I stayed.

When the new boat broke apart in an early round, he
left the Olympic Village,
moved into our four-mat guest room.
We could hear him weeping every night,
as he did his push-ups, sit-ups, crunches.

He skipped the closing ceremony
where the drunken young athletes of the world broke
ranks, jumped fences, cartwheeled across the field,
picked up the Japanese flag bearer and
carried him around the stadium,
tried to kiss every woman on the Japanese team;
removed and exchanged
clothing, embraced each other, invited spectators to join them,
refused to end the Games
as the loudspeakers repeated:
Will the athletes please march in ranks
Will the athletes please follow their nation's flags
in five languages.

II

I saw the Brazilian Olympic team
parade down Avenida Presidente Vargas
at midnight at *Carnaval,*
covered with gilt paint, feathers, rhinestones, mirrors.
Someone was hitting a hubcap with a little hammer;
they had flutes, whistles, bells, sticks, rattles;
one girl was bare-breasted, twirling in a half slip,
a light-skinned man shook a gourd with pebbles.
A few wore huge dildos and threatened the crowd with them.
Coke bottles, drums, singing;
    Cidade maravilhosa
tens of thousands of team members

streaming down from the Rio favelas
    Coração do meu Brasil
to dance, laughing, in the streets.

III

I have the most beautiful woman in Botafogo
sings the taxi driver.
Sunday, I will go to the beach and meet another.
Then I will have the two most beautiful women.
I will call them both Patricia.

IV

The Brazilian Olympic team stretches concrete arms on a hill
    above Rio;
eagles perch on its finger tips and scream to the new sun.
I must take Klaus here.
We will drink *cachaça,* and fly like eagles to the sea,
and call it a closing ceremony.

Christina's Fantasy

— After the Andrew Wyeth painting, *Christina's World*

They have carried her into the field again, under the sun.

She is lying there, and I, the watcher,
retreat within the dark within the room,
look past the straw-thin limbs
and picture us together, splayed across
the bed the sere dead grass provides.

There is the thrust and promise
of that hip, sensual as the soft
green and brown hills on the road to Querétaro,
folding, snuggled into one another,
the thick, smooth limbs of Zúñiga's women,
so out of order in this northern place.

He has arranged her in the field, under the faded sun.

And he, ascetic, handsomely detached,
provides her with a pale pink shift,
and his young wife's young body,
flanks swelling under the shift
and I, circling now like a hawk,
shall carry her beyond Querétaro
to where the hills become rich meadows.

I shall arrange her in those dark fields, under the full sun,
and she will blossom there, complete and warm.

Paul Delvaux's Women

Naked and silent,
they stroll the moonlit
small town Belgian streets,
eyes vacant,
somnambulists
gliding through train stations
and unexplained arcades.

Now they have followed me to Boston.
I stand dumb at the window
as lines of Flemish women
wearing only earrings,
small-breasted and
heavy-thighed,
flow slowly, noiselessly up Beacon Street.

Late yesterday some of them
crept through the wire north of Newton
into no-man's land.
Encountering a group of suburban housewives
they exchanged photographs,
kisses,
and fraternized throughout the night.

Gray plazas teem with their presence.
New squares have appeared
in the center of the city.
The women sit at small outdoor cafés
eating pastries, dots of cream on their lips,
bare legs touching,
smiling at some private joke.
Their fragrance surrounds my days.

Variation on a Theme by Marc Chagall

Imagine, then, a night of fog and damp
that saturates this quiet seaside patch
un-hip, unknown, above Miami Beach;
a string of low-rise, low-rent old motels
that squat between the shore and Route 1A,
a beachfront Promenade that thrums with restaurants,
joggers, bikers, walkers through the day
almost deserted now at half past ten:
some street lamps shimmer in the moist, warm air,
palms shuffle, surf retreats; a radio
plays music of another time and place.

Imagine, too, that dull sedans are gliding
to a halt on side streets near the beach;
odd shapes emerge, alone or paired, assembling
near the Promenade with whispered nods;
low greetings trill across the mist and darkness.
There is a small convergence here of women;
shapeless women, women in stiff wigs,
in skirts so long and large they sweep the ground,
in clothing that provides a sense of bulk.
These are Hasidic women, Lubavitche,
descendants of the *shtetl*, covered, swaddled,
a coven of the ultra-orthodox.

In this sun-crazed State they flee the sun;
in this land that treasures bodies, theirs
are hidden from all view; and yet the gentle
cries and giggles coming from the group
are growing louder, teasing, boisterous.
They mingle on stone benches now, bent forward,
preoccupied with something at their feet;
one at a time, like fledglings, each ascends
and smiles shyly, hesitant at first,
and then, six inches taller and beatific,
the coven is prepared to rollerblade.
In twos and threes, with arms outstretched and flailing,
with skirts swept back and flat against their thighs,
they balance as they practice navigation;
attempt to turn, then gather nerve and skill
and holding hands and laughing, floating, rolling,
in private darkness in a private world,
the Lubavitche women sail the Promenade.

Hexagram

An eruv is a bounded space within which Jews who adhere to
traditional religious law can "carry" objects in public spaces on
the Sabbath . . . Its boundary is a real physical entity . . . walls,
trees, telephone wires . . . lengths of twine.
— *The Community Eruv*

Among the ultra-Orthodox, the *eruv* line
surrounds a circumscribed community, confined
by fences, walls, and twisted lengths of plastic twine.
Here, the certitudes of God, of man and mind,
rotate and swirl about each other in a ring
of tightly argued logic; here, wise *rebbes* string

out meditations on the nature of each string
and knot that forms the *tzitzit:* kabbalistic line
of calculations follows line until the ring
of bearded mystics poking at each word can find
their truths and proofs. And here, though none have undermined
the Sabbath laws, the laws may deftly intertwine

and bend within the *eruv's* boundaries, as twine
will stretch to meet new needs. But Saturdays, the string
bikinis shining by the green-blue sea remind
observant boardwalk walkers that the *eruv* line
that runs along Miami Beach is less defined,
more serpentine; that here a woman's diamond ring

may navigate her waist and hips, that cell phones ring
on *Shabos*, almost-naked joggers sweat white wine.
Among the skull caps, curls and caftans, unrefined
turistas slouch: Latinos, Russians, gangsters. String-
thin Asian fashion models navigate their in-line
skates past beaver-hatted dandies; none pay mind

as women in their Hermès scarfs and *sheitel*s mind
long ranks of strollers. Further south, the nipple ring
personifies the Beach. The smoke, the toke, the line
of coke, the all-night clubs where genders can entwine
in every combination: now a gleaming string
of dancers roams the floor, and calls, and seeks to find

more players for a game that's not yet been defined—
but none here come here with Kabbala on their mind.
The *eruv* scene becomes a painting where a string
of half-mad sages link their arms to form a ring
around the moon. Freed from their bounds and binds of twine,
they rise like eagles, soaring in a graceful line.

And rapt with string, or drugs, or wine, their voices ring
across the earth-bound line. Can madmen help us find
that place where man and God and mind may intertwine?

Sketches from Route 1

1

FUCK MILK! GOT POT? a wall of T-shirts cries,
I'M SHIT-FACED ON DUVAL STREET IN KEY WEST
TELL YOUR BOOBS STOP STARING AT MY EYES
as here, in Paradise, their chests addressed
with poetry and flair, the young attest
to perfumed tropic air, the sun-drenched play
of light on sea, a primal, noble quest:
I LIKE TO EAT IT RAW LIKE HEMINGWAY
A string of crowded clam bars throbs in disarray.

2

A string of Ski-Doos throbs in disarray,
the ocean churned to iridescent green.
No comfort here for shades and depths of gray,
or those who think that swells of opaline
seem artificial, tinted, or obscene.
This sea is key-lime lime; the buildings blue,
canary, mauve, or pink—aquamarine—
and all that matters is an ocean view,
a lipo-sculptured body, and a bold tattoo.

3

Venceremos, reads the old tattoo
behind the bar on Calle Ocho Street
where men who once were men with guns now brew

café con leche, skim milk, Ultra Sweet.
On every other Thursday night they meet
above a grocery store, and ramble on
on politics, betrayal and deceit;
the summer breezes off the Malecón;
how dolphins and a fisherman saved Elian.

4

No talk of fishermen or Elian
invades the Palm Beach *Palm*, where well-aged meat
is all that counts: blood-red chateaubriand
will make this gray- and white-haired crowd complete.
This is no place for vegans; the effete
are not among the well-tanned coterie
that chatters here, bejeweled and indiscrete.
The Palm Beach *Palm* exudes prosperity;
a scent of flesh and freshly oiled mahogany.

5

A regal sense of dark mahogany;
thick drapes obscure all views of sun or sand;
cut glass and jade, chinoiserie; and she—
straight-backed at ninety-three—will take a stand!
They plan to raze her building, and demand
she leave. But she shall float above the beach—
her rugs, TV, her *tchotchkes* close at hand—
twenty stories high, where seagulls screech,
suspended by pure will, she hangs beyond their reach.

6

Suspended by a dream beyond your reach,
you hang above this land—forevermore
El Chulo—Ponce, you pimp, you half-pint leech,
you cockamamy, cracked conquistador;
you soul, you fairy queen, you metaphor
for all the fools who choose to fantasize
that God rolls dice along this sun-crazed shore.
We've fallen for your whispering, your lies!
I'VE FOUND ETERNAL YOUTH a wall of T-shirts cries.

Still Life

At HARBOUR VILLAGE HOUSE the AGE remains,
scabrous in Miami's evening light;
a goodbye wink, a kiss to end the night.
The letters, palimpsests of hints and stains,
adorn the old facade, obscured among
fresh banners that proclaim that on this site
a string of towers, glass and malachite,
will be constructed for the Always Young.

And stretching to the north along the beach
are thirty-story slabs in raw concrete;
monolithic, empty, incomplete,
construction halted, future out of reach.
Around these vast, abandoned blocks of gray
the rebar-cluttered sands stretch far away.

Overheard at Park and Fifty-Third

"My name is Asia, by the way," she says,
after trading kisses with a brown-
and beige-clad blonde whose muted, silken tones
are counterpoints to Asia's pin-striped suit.
The Avenue has changed: the young now thrust
themselves upon the scene as if they owned
the air and sky, and crowds of brisk professionals
go sweeping by, androgynous and swift.

First the friendship kiss, and then the name?
That seems to be the way it's done these days—
old rules all tossed aside, new icons raised.
The Seagram Building looks diminished, lost
among the bold new neighbors that define
this city I no longer can call mine.

Navajo Country

Coming into this place the land is mostly
dun-colored, empty, wind-torn and crazed;
pancaked beer cans punctuate the roadside.
Here and there communities sit loosely,
shadowed only by the clouds,
and what there is of them is linear;
the part that matters to a traveler
stretched along the single street
that pulls off from the interstate
to there and back.

Cement-block buildings and some single-wides,
the reservation-owned convenience store.
Doritos, Fritos, Sugar Snacks,
Twinkies, Cheese Whirls, jerky sticks.
A thick and buffalo-looking man buys smokes.
Some teenage girls with angry skin
are talking family with a tribal cop.
Two backboards, crooked hoops, a grassless square.

Thirty miles north the earth convulses;
striations, dull red walls, Giacometti
figures carved into the overhangs of cliffs,
whispers of an ochre world where gods assemble
stone on stone, and then a plaza by De Chirico,
swept clean
scrabbled slate surrounded by three walls of rock.
A twisted, barren piñon angles toward the sky.
Shape-shifters, owls, ghosts, coyote bones,
shadows gather in the slanting light.
An hour more to Farmington.

Two Love Stories

Her Princeton MFA, his partnership.
A turquoise choker with a silver clasp,
two Breuer chairs, an aunt's pied-à-terre,
a Baskin woodblock print. An opening
at Sotheby's, a brightly patterned vest,
a small tattoo, the scent of cloves, cocaine.
A nose once mangled in a rugby match.
The Parthenon, Antarctica, Beijing.

Her denim wedding skirt, his Zuni blood,
a way of always laughing after sex.
Two spotted dogs, a uniform, a cat
that jumps on stranger's laps, some paperbacks.
A chance to leave the *pueblo* far behind.
A neatly folded flag, a body bag.

Awaiting Departure

The four-hundred-pound man in the Departure Lounge
wears an oversized black shirt and broad black pants
that follow loosely as he shifts around,
a damp, white towel sifting through his hands.
Tented in his shrouds, he moves invisibly;
it is impossible to tell if they contain
a structure solid as a side of beef,
or rolls of moisture, odor and decay.

No one takes a bench seat near this man,
or chats with him about delays; no one
will catch his eye, or chance an indication
he exists; but as each flight call sounds
the sideways glances flutter, just a check;
the cause unmentioned, and the fear unsaid.

Prologue

This is the calm that calms the fools,
the quiet eye that does not blink,
the blade set bare before the storm.

This is the famous hall of sighs
where whispers cling to walls and run
the circle of the sweating stone.

This is the cancer, hiding from light;
the dead still sea, the silent wind;
this is the calm that melts your bones.

Here now the idols carved into rock,
churches and graveyards, blisters on skin,
ice-covered beaches pale in the moon.

This is the prologue; here now the beast.

III.

Buying Sneakers

Penelope Lunches With Friends

I weave and weave, and then at night unweave—
at least that's how we set it up for show.
Amazing, love, what people will believe.

The suitors suit me fine. No need to grieve.
I just can't sleep alone, and *comme il faut*
I'll weave a tale; and then all night I weave

from man to man to man without reprieve.
It's cock and bull and cocks and balls, and so
amazing, love, what people will believe

when all I want from life's the breathe and heave
of one strong beau above and one below:
I weave and weave, and late at night when we've

all come and they're all gone I might achieve
a sense of peace, and dream about some slow,
amazing love. What people will believe

is what will count, not what I do. Deceive
the geezer and I'm set, so let him know
I weave and weave, and then at night unweave.
Amazing, love, the myths they will believe.

Buying Sneakers

> The designer's iconic plaid on this canvas high top lace-up
> sneaker ($275) is hand sprayed to give it a slight dégradé effect.
> — Advertisement in the *New York Times*

The look I want is slightly *dégradé*;
aloof and elegant, yet with a flair
that hints of darkness in an offhand way;

exquisite, yes, but not too *recherché*,
and at the same time, more than *ordinaire*.
That look! I want it *slightly dégradé*,

just right to make the scene in St. Tropez,
or stir up gossip of an old *affaire*
with hints of darkness and the offhand way

that one once murmured, *je suis désolée*,
and left a lover twisting in the air.
The look is wan, and *jeune*, and *dégradé*.

Now that my Nikes have become *passé*,
I need a *soupçon* of aggrieved despair
that hints of darkness in an offhand way,

so show me something that is *distingué*,
that cries *regardez-moi*, and makes you dare
to look. And want me slightly *dégradé*!
I hint at darkness in an offhand way.

Buster and Etta

Buster's father raised the boy to shoot
right for the goal: "Act like a man, and toe the line,
but never be a grind"—and Buster learned to wear
the Princeton colors, played lacrosse and squash, interned
at Haversham & Hayes—there was no yes or no
about the MBA, or joining father's bank.

Etta grew up near the river bank,
in the kind of shotgun shack a man could shoot
a 12-gauge through—and her daddy let folks know
he'd done that once or twice. He couldn't draw a line
she wouldn't cross, but Etta turned out tall and slim, and turned
sixteen aboard a silver bus to anywhere.

Buster found his niche in Major Clients where
he handles downtown types. Their Left Bank,
left-wing prattle and their politics can turn
his stomach, but it's business. He'd rather shoot
some billiards at the Club, yet strangely can't malign
a kind of life he finds, at times, he wants to know.

Etta dishes with new friends: "The pants come off, you know,
and like, her father's name is on his underwear!"
Super-model, twenty-two, she stalks the runway line;
a lion queen, the next new thing, a fashion passion bank.
The crowd applauds her stylish strut, while all she thinks is, "Shoot,
somewhere out there's a real man," and keeps her face upturned.

Now Buster flies to Nassau, where he'll leave no stone unturned,
in a weekend planned for rugby, and for girls who won't say *No*.
And Etta's off to Tangiers on a five-day photo shoot;
she rustles through her *shmattes* as she picks out what to wear.
Her limo passes Buster's just as his departs the bank,
by the time they stop at JFK their orbits both align.

She buys a skim milk latte; Buster's next in line.
He is on a cell phone; her trim back is turned.
Etta glides right past him; Buster texts the bank.
Buster looks so handsome; Etta doesn't know.
They never get together, though they crisscross everywhere;
and leave on different aircraft, with their future down the chute.

Etta turned to chic design, and had her own sleek line.
Or did she turn to drugs and booze, and cocaine line-by-line?
The bank went bust and Buster lost his golden parachute.
Or did, in time, he run the bank, with time to hunt and shoot?
There may be still more endings, and you've got to be aware:
One never knows where life will go, or how or when or where.

Retired, and Living in Seclusion Near Las Vegas, Khan Reflects

"What I miss mostly is the Golden Horde—
my Mongol guys—I'll tell you, we could ride
all day and night! That year our horsemen roared
across the steppes, the West was terrified.
And us? We were the mother-humping pride
of Asia, baby. The pussy Bulgars flung
their spears away and ran like rats and died.
That was the life! Bows all tightly strung,
the wind like knives, the ponies strong. We were so young!"

The old barbarian dabs away a tear,
takes some time to readjust his shawl,
and waits to catch his breath. It's pleasant here—
his books, his row of axes on the wall;
his handsome wife now joins us, blonde and tall.
"Brandi was dancing at the Desert Inn.
At first she didn't go for me at all,
but Mongols always find a way to win."
She pours herself some tonic, and a ton of gin.

"I'm still pissed-off that John Wayne played me,"
he goes on. "The Duke's a *mensch*—I love the man—
but I deserved that role! The studio made me
give in—they said that I was shorter than
the part required, that their asshole fan
base liked its asshole heroes six foot four.

Technical Advisor was a sham
to keep me quiet, but we're still at war.
I've been around a long time, and I know the score.

"*And* they screwed me on the royalties.
And points! What do I know from gross and net?
I learned to fight and kill, not deal with sleaze!
I'll make them eat their own intestines yet!"
"He's tired," Brandi says. "And maybe wet."
She ends the interview. I say that's fine
and mutter that I'm very glad we've met.
We hug goodbye; her fingers play with mine.
"He takes his pills at eight," she breathes. "Come back at nine."

Caveat Emptor

The Plaza merchants spot their fashion victim—
turquoise-encrusted huntress, silver-lined,
all planes and features deftly redefined
by knife and Botox to the latest dictum.
They sing to her with whispering conviction:
Come see, the finest gem stones ever mined,
or tribal rugs, incredibly refined.
These treasures can become your next addiction!

Coyote tips his chair back, stretches, preens—
his instincts tell him that she's on her own,
has sensed his presence and will venture near,
inspect his Stetson brim and leather jeans.
He eyes her perfect breasts, her skin, her tone—
Is this seat taken? God, he loves it here!

Her Latest Girlfriend Stole the Silk Tabriz and Left a Cat Behind

And so, she lives apart, slim and austere,
among adobe walls of mauve and plum;
Tibetan prayer flags sway in cool dawn air,
their shadows skirl about her sleeping room.
She takes Ashtanga yoga twice a week,
meditates, brews pale green tea each night;
the Dalai Lama beams upon a desk
that sits between two bookshelves: her retreat.
And, now and then, she'll take a hike alone,
or ski, or see a film, or simply drive
at dusk through shades of hills and twisted pine
to watch the moon escape an ancient cliff:
and wonder why she needs to try again
to be a judge of women, or of men.

Dinner at the Inn of the Anasazi

She deals in high-end artifacts, and so
that flash of bright responsive smile might be
sincere—you cannot tell—but one can see
the tension there; a sense of Jeanne Moreau.
At fifty plus, both age and beauty show,
the black skirt hides a belly: her worldliness—
the eyes that know more than they want to know—
is tempered by quick glances that address
a husband's back: his boyish postures press
her clients over drinks. *My wife loves sales,*
and that's her life, but I define success
as time for me. Do you ski the Taos trails?
She strokes his neck—he flinches—and spilled wine
incarnadines the linen's Zapotec design.

A Brighton Beach Princess Remembers the Past

Brighton Beach, the largest Russian community in the
United States, is sometimes called *Odessa by the Sea*.
— *New York Aspects,* Kingsbridge Davidson Press

Was it peasants or pheasant I found so unpleasant?
I remember a grand, open-back touring car—
a family reunion when I, prepubescent,
was photographed next to a large samovar;
a man with long hair and blue eyes—incandescent—
my sisters and Mama; my father the Czar.

But all of these images turn deliquescent,
as useless and putrid as bad caviar,
when I think of the guns, and a strangely incessant
girl's screaming, a cellar, men shooting, a scar.

Mother Russia still beckons, her soul effervescent,
like champagne that swallowed a bright shooting star;
but I have my boardwalk, my Bingo, the present—
pelmeni for dinner—and the past seems so far.

Jane

He had an ex, as men his age all do;
an actress, self-involved and quite insane,
he said, but it was over now with Jane,
or so he said, as men his age will do
(at least, the ones she was attracted to),
but there was something there that pulled her chain—
a sense of humor, and a half a brain.
He cooked, they talked, he knew the books she knew,
and rapt with who each was and what they'd read,
they drained the wine and tumbled into bed.

She had this errant gene, she liked to say,
which went back to the time when men began
and kicked in every time she met a man
as smart as she (friends joked about the way
that even after too much chardonnay,
she never could admit to "smarter than"),
she'd sleep with him, fall half in love, and plan
a brand new life—then find out he was gay,
(at least unstraight), or slightly undivorced,
or only liked it when the sex was forced.

But this time all went well, if all unschemed:
she had her crazies, sure, but so did he;
even the neuroses nestled perfectly.
She loved the way his sunburst neckties gleamed

against dark business suits; their tastes all seemed
the same—*the dishes even matched*—and she
began to get the sense that possibly
this one might work; the voice that often screamed
beware was almost still, and she felt good
about herself in ways she rarely could.

There was a problem, though, in that he clung
to memories of Jane: he'd reminisce
about some role she'd played; then try to twist
the conversation when he saw he'd stung
her—when she cried—but Jane's old stills still hung
along a hallway, and he clearly missed
that glamour he had shared, the show biz glitz.
So, slowly, as she settled in among
the shreds of Jane, she moved them out of sight:
the stills and posters went without a fight.

In time Jane disappeared, as ex-wives do,
and life evolved to whiskers in the drain,
and tedium, or sometimes some champagne,
and him and her, and nothing to pursue
now that they had each other. He just withdrew,
he shrank, and then it hit her like a train
that everything he was was formed by Jane.
The dishes, books, his earthy *pot-au-feu*
were Jane's; the neckties she adored a gift
from Jane; without Jane he was cast adrift.

He bought himself some ties, striped shades of brown,
and she exchanged them—Christ, they were *passé*—
for golden splashes like a summer day,
and he was fine with that. He settled down,
and let her run their life without a frown.
She caught Jane in a new off-Broadway play,
and introduced herself, and later they
talked hours, in a place Jane knew downtown.
She understood, but couldn't quite explain,
that what she'd done was fall in love with Jane.

Where Are the Negligees of Anthony?

My closet still holds forty pin-striped suits
arranged in shades and grades of blue and gray—
each morning I compare their attributes:
The peaked lapels to see the bank, today?
That muted chalk from Nathan Road should play
well there—the Savile Row's too rich, I fear.
But bright new days now only bring dismay:
where are the clothes of yesteryear?

A businessman must have his absolutes,
those vested interests he will not betray:
I flaunt my Turnbull ties and Magli boots;
this banker favors skin-snug jeans that sway
each time she moves, and whispers, "Call me Kay."
But when I squeeze her knee, and call her "dear,"
she calls the loan—and knocks my hand away.
Where are the suits of yesteryear?

They're gone, all gone, on golden parachutes,
to seek the sun and gargle chardonnay;
and what they've left behind as substitutes
are brutes, in wrinkled chino disarray,
who think that style's a Harvard MBA
and T-shirts that promote some brand of beer.
Oh, every day these days is Casual Day.
Where are the clothes of yesteryear?

Bespoken yet unspoken for, I stay,
aware that reinforcements won't appear,
and know that when they throw me out they'll say:
He wore the clothes of yesteryear.

IV.

There Was a Woman Once

Never Mind

He wondered what was meant by "never mind,"
and whether all the laughter in her eyes
was there for him, and if they'd ever find
which parts of each were real and which disguised

disguises and constraints that led them both
to wonder what was meant by "never mind."
And as she turned away his fingers rose
to brush her shoulder, paused, and sent a kind

of brief communication which combined
detachment and concern, and somehow made
her wonder what she'd meant by "never mind,"
and what the game was now, and how one played.

He gestured vaguely toward her, while she
considered what "whatever" signified,
and touched a finger to him, carefully.
He wondered what she meant by "never mind."

Crossing Brooklyn Bridge At Night

They seem a tightly balanced pair, suspension
bridges and their rivers; a marriage where
one partner hangs mid-air and trembles, tension
manifest in tics and sighs, but there—
below—the other, darker, deeper lies.

Summer Island

You sit outside, consorting with your wine
as I, inside, consider what to say
or do to try to redefine the line
you sit outside. Consorting with your wine
now seems your choice; and solitude is mine,
and neither works to overcome the way
you sit outside, consorting with your wine
as I, inside, consider what to say.

Pretty *Gaijin* Boys Have Often Been Her Weakness

This one smells so sweet
And sour—like *takuan* pickles—
Her pretty silly
Gaijin daikon pickle boy
She stretches as he strokes her

      Oh God, he thinks, this is incredible:
      he has to find the time to write them all
      I met this geisha girl, and now she's curled
      up with me in my room in Tokyo,
      here at the old Hotel Imperial.

Pretty *gaijin* boys
Have often been her weakness
That and the brandy
And *danna-san* off golfing
In Hakone with his wife

      Yanagibashi geishas, he'd been told;
      very famous and traditional.
      But most were old. And then the casual
      hand upon his thigh, a squeeze, a bold
      but private look, a number on a card.

Such luck to find him
A boring Daiwa party
After shall we meet?
She glided through the lobby
Panties folded in her sleeve

They spent the morning making love again,
and still he could not quite believe that she
was real—she had been dressed so carefully,
kimono purple, golden sash, and then,
with all that silk, no underwear, just skin.

No more time to play
The Fuji Bank reception
Starts at six she must
Instruct the maids and dancers
First some lunch with *daikon-boy*

He's never used the hotel sushi bar;
the sweep of pine, the rows of lacquer trays,
so Japanese. *I don't eat fish,* he says,
but shrimp's okay, and nuzzles at her ear,
then runs his fingers through the just-brushed hair.

Sushi Master Jun
Knows her from Yoshiwara
Suggests fat tuna
Streaked with white. *And for your friend?*
She requests the dancing shrimp.

Raw shrimp, alive and writhing, are now spread
behind the counter, heads and shells stripped clean,
the bodies dipped in soy and served to him.
He watches each one quiver, armor shed,
too dumb to know it is already dead.

Two Tales from the East

The women in the prints of Utamaro
are quiet, self-involved
with dress and style
Their faces bear an air of inner sorrow
They do not smile

    Unexpectedly
    At Fifth and Sixty-second
    Old Tokyo lover
    Tea house owner, former geisha
    Waiting for the light to change

    An Hermès scarf waves
    "I am with my Italian
    Banker friend, we are
    Staying here, at the Pierre.
    Such a small world, is it not?"

    Twenty years ago
    Sharing the first noodle bowl
    New Year's tradition
    At Nanzenji, in the hills
    Snow on a yellow obi

Emerging from the bath or at a mirror
their beauty is dissolved

in time and place
The soul of *ukiyoe* is an aura
of whispered grace

Mink coat, winter tan
Her hair is fox-toned red now
"But he is away.
I am sad bachelor girl
Left all alone in New York."

Bare tatami *room*
Chilly morning at the inn
Gray light on shoji
Sounds of chimes and temple bells
Her cool skin smooth as the straw

Restructured eyelids
Frosted lipstick, matching nails
"Perhaps we can meet.
Do you know Piano Bar Jun?"
In her bag a cell phone rings

These willow trees one sees in Yoshiwara
transplanted, will resolve
to stay alive
become invasive, grab for air and moisture
They grow and thrive

In the Spring of 1978

It is Saturday morning,
so we sleep in late,
and eat cold Chinese takeout for breakfast,
eventually emerge blinking out onto East 53rd,
to walk over to the Museum
in time for the 1:40 Kurosawa film.
She notices Marcelle a half block ahead,
good forty-year-old legs and thighs
showing well in a tight skirt.
"Her ass is getting fat," she says.
"Is that what you screw these days," she says,
 "Catherine Deneuve with a big ass?"

The Festival goes on forever:
Akahige today, I think.
Last time we did this we ran into one of her
old Shinjuku boyfriends, Peter Stern, and his entire
Far Eastern Studies class in from Princeton
via Port Authority, and we all had *zaru soba*
together later on Ninth Avenue while she
played Lady Murasaki; but now is today and
today is hot for May, even the breeze
off the river at our backs is hot,
you can smell the city,
almost taste the river,

and we are going to see a Kurosawa.
"I don't know why," she says, "but it seems like Tokyo today."

It does.
It feels like drifting through Okachimachi on a Saturday,
checking out the fish displayed at every stall,
fingering the matsutake mushrooms, buying *oden* from a wagon,
listening for the *"Yaaaakiimo!"* bleat of the roast-sweet-potato guy.

We stop for hot dogs at the Sabrett cart,
where there is already a line.
I recognize Roy Lichtenstein,
and she spots Jasper Johns.

For Trudy, in New York on Business

You came and went in dead flat Hopper light:
encounter at the Whitney; swift affair
that we, both married, knew would lead nowhere—
but all each wanted was the one-night
stand of sorts; late afternoon-lit flight
to your hotel; a lamp, a desk, a chair,
a bed on which to stumble, fall and share
the satisfaction of an appetite

for unexpected sex. No mysteries,
no chiaroscuro worked to mask the sight
of loose and mottled flesh. And did we care?
Was there more there than Edward Hopper sees?
You filled the window, stark, unshaded, bright;
I watched your shadow paint the soot-choked air.

Looking Back

The way the marriage worked was she would paint
from midnight until six am, and he
would rise as she slid into bed, and she
would sleep past noon, and wake, and reacquaint
herself with friends, and smile without complaint
as he came home too late each night; and he
was no more bothered by their life than she,
for neither cared that either was no saint.

Or so the story went—the one he told
to women he encountered now and then,
and polished with each use, then used again—
devised to snare the curious or bold.
It worked so well that finally he forgot
which parts of it were true and which were not.

The Performer

She met a man of strange but charming skills,
who entertained by juggling champagne corks
as he squared three-digit numbers in his head;
who opened breakfast eggs one-handed, never
smashed a yolk—*I don't like pigeonholes,*
he said, and practiced yoga, quoted Marx,
did crosswords with a Montblanc fountain pen—
her friends all said he was extremely clever.

But he had a problem recognizing
patterns—or a woman's waiting face—
or recalling what he'd said some other time.

He worked a brand new trick with eggs and plates
the day she left; distressed she would not see
their perfect and unbroken symmetry.

A Game of *Go*

So like the combat in a game of *Go*,
this quiet drama, played between the *shoji* screens
of almost empty rooms. Imagine new
tatami mats, their sweet, fresh reeds still touched with green;
the smell of straw, young pine and tea;
a low and graceful table, cushions, you and me
exchanging claim and counterclaim:
what better way to end it than a game?

We shall encase ourselves in white *yukatas;*
the starched and just-unfolded cotton straight and stiff;
sit back upon our heels, hands on thighs—
two actors in an *ukiyoe* print—then with
the brisk, quick moves we know by heart,
set out the bowls and hollowed board; and bow, and start:
each click of stone on *kaya* wood
a sound that cannot be misunderstood.

There was another, younger life, when *chess*
was where we fought and loved; when we would slash diagonals
across each other's path, and stop and kiss
in midnight, all-night coffee shops for every captured piece.
The game we played involved baroque
and public risk; you laughed, and draped your hair to cloak
each move; and I would feint, slide back,
pretend that I was hurt—and then attack.

Now *Go* avoids emotion, has no crowd,
no court, no courtiers, no ruined and toppled queens;
we face a flat and square and hard-ruled board
where pieces, black and white, entwine and interweave—
and some are yours, and some are mine,
and who owns what, or whom, is what we must define.
It's not to conquer, but *possess:*
simpler, and yet more intricate than chess.

There Was a Woman Once

Unavoidably, in Delft, Delft blue;
and Bruges was mostly dark canals and white
lace antimacassars; she made me eat
moules for the first time, we both learned to drink
the amber Flemish beers and, thinking back,
there was a woman once, and she was tall.

There was a woman once and she was tall;
radiant, in an awkward way, with blue
eyes set too far apart, but her naked back
felt like silk, and her short-cropped, near-white
street waif hair looked swell behind a drink,
but what we liked to do the most was eat.

And what we liked to do the most was eat
our way across Manhattan; she was tall,
and life was good, the sex and food and drink
were good—weekends, sometimes, we'd hit the Blue
Note down on Hudson, hip crowd, black and white,
and we left something there we can't get back.

And there was something there we can't get back,
but what we liked to do the most was eat;
that time in Kyoto, the *shoji* screens all white,
there was a woman there, and she was tall;
grilled squid, the platter glazed dark-brown and blue,
hot *saké,* served in little cups, the drink.

Hot *saké,* served in little cups, to drink,
and there was something there we can't get back,
a sense of loss, unreachable and blue,
but what we liked we liked the most was eat.
There was a woman once, and she was tall,
her eyes were Baltic blue, her hair was white.

Her pretty eyes were blue, her hair was white.
Hot *saké* served in little cups to drink.
There was a woman once, and she was tall.
And something there was there we can't get back.
But what we liked to do the most was eat.
Her hair white, white, so pretty eyes blue blue.

A woman once, go back, her eyes blue blue.
Her she so white, so tall, we loved drink eat.
Blue, white, back, drink, eat, eat, tall, tall tall tall.

V.

Life in the Second Circle

What Would the Wind Drive?

What kind of car would the wind drive?
— Question at a poetry workshop

The Wind once rode a big black, badass Hawg,
a twisted blue bandanna on his head:
tattooed and sleeveless; lean, mean junkyard dog.

Now every flaming-asshole-walking-dead
executive has got hisself a bike:
middle-aged accountants dress alike
in stiff new leather gear, with *HARLEY* splashed
across their backs. The Wind stays home. Unwed,
alone, he surfs the net for porn instead
of cruising roads; eats Sugar Corn Pops stashed
beneath the bed; or sits and smokes his dope.

He thinks to buy some sneakers, join a group
that walks most mornings at the mall. He'll cope,
he says, and opens up a can of soup.

Life in the Second Circle

I live on a beach with a woman who hates pigeons.
This is not the Piazza di
Popoli she yells, pegging salt-swept stones

at them: I share a house with Anna Magnani—she
emerged sad-eyed, years back, from an out-of-date
old film cassette, talking too much, absurdly

big red mouth bursting with kisses: all that first night
we loved and laughed and spoke of life, and she devoured
my grilled squab *puttanesca* with a whore's bold appetite.

We live in cinematic garlic-spatteredness, my hard-
life love and I, with recondite Fellini dreams
and black-and-white De Sica screens—the outside world

can't reach this beach. *"They all are pigeons,"* Anna screams.
"Their asses spread, they flap their wings, their shit is everywhere."
We tumble to the kitchen floor; make love amidst tomato streams.

Aubadergine

Awakening, I still can taste your flesh,
the soul contained within the supple
skin you wear, voluptuous and purple.
I have been warned you are the path to madness
and yet, despite the crumbs and salt that kiss
and linger on my lips, there is no brutal
morning-after sting; but just the sweet and subtle
whisper of a roasted scrap, a speck of crust;
a bitter lemon and the scent of thyme;
the rapture of the olive grove, and you as mine.

Renate

The smell of petrol and the sound of tanks
was where it started, then the flight, and lines
of cars and wagons moving, moving, moving,
looking for some space between the guns.
And when it ended they were moved again,
from camp to camp, until her father paid
a man to make and stamp their documents.

She learned some words of English on the boat,
and then learned more; a large and quiet girl
who always wore the same long dress to class.
In time she chanced a kind of solemn smile.
An oddly adult girl, she disremembered
other lives, absorbed this new one page-by-page,
curled in a nest behind a folding screen;
and as her parents worked and slept and worked
she found her way into a different world.

So when she met him—backgrounds similar,
but different—*We all got out in thirty-six*—
and his mother hugged her, led her into their
immense apartment, over-stuffed with noise and family,
she hugged back; and from the start she never knew
if it was him or Libby whom she chose to hug.

      · · · · ·

She left a note for him when Libby phoned—
Your mother called to say we had four kids—
fought off the wise-ass urge to say, "No shit?
I guess we both forgot—I'll tell him now—
you think that we should call off the divorce?"
hung up on Libby—wrote the stupid note—
and cried, then cried and giggled, quite alone
and frightened; but fell asleep aware of how
all that they had left together was
Your mother called to say we had four kids.

And watched him leave, looked up a lawyer she
had flirted with at parties some time back,
and fought and won to keep the house and kids—
but then there was support, and all the tax
returns, and his and hers, and blah-blah-blah,
and somewhere there she waved a small white flag;
just found a job and raised the brood—withdrew
into her garden and her yellow house—
and drank too much, and wept when bills were due,
but always knew she had her house and kids.

Life being life, the bitch it wants to be,
they ran into each other now and then
at school events, or when, one at a time,
she'd drop off kids for weekends spent with him
and sometimes see a woman—younger, slim,
with olive skin—who nodded awkwardly.

She never asked the four a thing, and they
said little, walked some private line; and when
she had to deal with him she was terse,
and told herself the house and kids were hers.

She found a better job, and then one more—
and fed and clothed them all, and paid enough
on every credit card to keep herself afloat.
Each Mother's Day an Irish woman came
to tend the kids, and she would drive alone
for hours down Cape Cod until the end of land
to find a hotel there, and walk the shore,
to look in windows on Commercial Street,
to buy a precooked lobster and good wine
and have them slowly, slowly, in her room.

      · · · · ·

So life went on. And one would like to say
she met another man and settled down
to watch the kids have grandkids as a knot
within her softened. Remained observant,
pensive, challenging, but not afraid
to hoot with joy at something that delighted her,
that life grew sweet—and some of that occurred.
She has her house, the walls are thick and dry,
it's in her name, the kids and grandkids call;
and yet on quiet mornings she still thinks
she smells the petrol, and can hear the tanks.

Because She Fell Out of Her Yoga Pose

She blamed herself, and quickly felt the shame
arise that went with blaming—self-critique,
because she could not cleanse her mind of blame,

had now erased the state of grace that came
from flowing pose to pose—she chewed her cheek,
and blamed herself and, *thinking*, felt the shame

that undermined the clean and simple aim
of *being where you are*—began to speak
because she could not cleanse her mind of blame—

and sensed on all the mirrored walls the same
refracted, anxious face, and took a peek,
and saw herself and quickly felt her shame

pervade the class, and struggled to reclaim
a sense of inner peace, but week by week,
because she could not cleanse her mind, her blame

became its own asana in this game
she always played alone; upset and bleak
she blamed herself and, blaming, felt the shame
because she could not cleanse her mind of blame.

Watchful Waiting

For men past fifty, guidelines indicate
a probing and a PSA each year—
a moment's pause while life is put on hold.
So once again my doctor, Brandon Wu,
inserts a latexed digit—but this time
encounters *something*—and we're even now
for all those years of "BRANDON, OH GOD, BRANDON,
BRANDON, YES! I WANT TO BEAR YOUR CHILDREN!"
For generations past of neat, unsmiling Wus
who paid for passage here on sailing ships
to lay the railroad tracks, and serve the food,
and work as clerks, and run a store, and save
to send a sad-eyed student east to Brown—
so he could find this fucking thing in me—
their purpose here on earth has been fulfilled.
"We've got you by the prostate," Brandon breathes,
his finger up my ass, and tongues my ear;
Old man, you're gonna die, you're gonna die,
then stands, laconic, blows away the smoke
that clouds his digit, twirls and holsters it.

Past seventy, the experts all will state,
watchful waiting is the way to go—
when PSA is relatively low,
the odds are something else will kill you first.
Statistically, that is. My heart may burst,

or lungs or kidneys fail, I'll have a stroke—
an angry horse can kick me in the head—
there're accidents and terrorists and plague,
and at your age we hate to operate.
The protocols serenely advocate
to wait—and watch my brand new, brash new friend—
to call him little Brandon, if I wish,
and go to ball games with him, and get drunk.
He'll be the son I never had, a bright young lad.
Makes sense. Statistically. Except, of course,
that I had planned on immortality,
and cannot sleep, because I fear my baby boy
has got an ice ax stashed beneath his bed.
He lies awake himself, and watches, waits—
but biopsies cause pain, and carry risk
as needles tear at flesh and snip-snip-snip—
supine among my cells, at home, entwined,
and aims a finger at my head, malignantly;
Old man, you're gonna die, you're gonna die.
He cantillates while strangers count my cells,
and then—the air now suddenly benign—
my little Brandon shrugs, and disappears.

At the Crafts Museum at Asheville

The willow twigs that shape a basket's base
twist and roam across each other's path
as man and woman, husband, handsome wife

navigate the halls and quiet spaces,
weave through groups of dulcimers complex
and elegant as praying mantises;

past wood, hemp, paper, clay; past quilts and shawls.
We drift together, chat in whispers,
wander off; to reunite from time to time

inside these rooms that smell of straw and leather,
iron, ash. *Pewter has a special scent,* I say,
and so do earthenware and stone;

inhale, eyes closed, and am at once outside
a *shoji* shop in Kyoto, fresh pine shavings
scattered in the street. I smell the trace of oil

in the air where leather once was worked,
ascend a cobbled Florence square; and floating,
floating, find myself again in Asheville,

admiring elemental, unglazed bowls.
The footfalls are my wife's, come round again;
her spiced perfume, the jade and silver pieces

on her ears, familiar yet discomforting
inside this place of dirt, air, fire, water,
man and gods—of potter's fingers scraping

for the truth within an unformed mass.
Has she been somewhere else? I never know.
Relationships are much like implements—

form follows function, function form—
and as we near the open door, I sense
the clash of evening and a taste of rain.

Watching Reruns

The weary talk, the crime scene tape, the crowd—
you've seen it all—and then we recognize
the taciturn offender, still unbowed,

who treats the evidence with feigned surprise
although it seems that we've been here before,
have seen it all, and then we recognize

a snatch of dialogue, a look, and more—
half-remembered moments, half-obscure
although it seems that we've been here before.

"I think we've seen this crap, but I'm not sure."
"It works much better if you stay awake."
Half-remembered moments, half-obscure,

filled with pretense for the story's sake;
the two of you, the screen, the same old plot,
"It works much better if you stay awake."

And there's another in the next time slot:
the weary talk, the crime scene tape, the crowd—
the two of you, the screen, the same old plot:
the taciturn offender, still unbowed.

Muhammad Ali Entered My Dream
Just to Say Hello

We talked mostly pussy,
two old guys trading brags and stories
old style, toe-to-toe, center of the ring,
nobody taking a backward step.
BAM! *Nothing on under the dress* BAP!
POP-POP-POP *then her other sister* BING!
Folks could hear them yelling my name POW!
and by about the fourth round
I was in trouble, mouth breathing, arm punches,
couldn't match his speed and moves
You can get them little motor homes to rocking
and all that joy and beauty.

So I switched to boxing,
told him how I saw him win the Golden Gloves,
delicious Cassius Clay from Louisville
seventeen years young
taking apart some gnarly old British semipro;
and we talked about Manila and Sonny Banks
and Cleveland Big Cat Williams and Sonny Liston
on his back in Maine
and eventually, of course, about that night in Zaire
with big George Foreman BOOM-BOOM-BOOM-BOOM
pounding him into the ropes in the eighth round,

Ali absorbing it all
(helped by those loose ropes),
then sliding off to SNAP a jab, and SNAP-SNAP
two more, and WHAP, a right, and WHAP-WHAP-WHAP-
   WHAP until
big George Foreman
destroyer of men, pulverizer of Joe Frazier,
choking on spiders,
toppled.

He told me about losing the title to Leon Spinks,
and getting into shape and winning it back,
and the crazy fight in Tokyo with the Japanese wrestler
who kicked the life out of his legs,
and how he came back from that to knock out Larry Holmes,
to win his fourth title, to be The Greatest Ever.
I couldn't bring myself to tell him
that he lost the Holmes fight,
that he was so badly beat up that twice
Holmes begged the referee to stop it
before he killed a man,
and that finally the corner threw in a white towel.
How could I say anything?
It was only a dream and it was his dream now also,
inside my dream of that beautiful seventeen-year-old boy
dancing in circles in Madison Square Garden
BAP-BAP-BAP-BAP-POW!

The River Children Come of Age

Those first years we lived above the river,
Christ, we were insatiable,
screwing our heads off in the kitchen,
on that floor you stenciled yellow,
and gave no thought to children
or the future, or the dead;

and, indeed, the dead
in time came to the river,
and the ghosts of children,
demanding and insatiable,
calling for that yellow
kitchen

within this new six-burner steel kitchen
where everything that lives is dead,
and a silent cat stares through slits of yellow,
and its owners fear the river;
and only the night is insatiable,
and there are no children;

and the friends who laughed like children
as we caressed each other's spouses in the kitchen,
six of us, one Christmas night, stoned and insatiable,
they are all dead, those others, dead;
the last one buried somewhere upstate near a river
last October, on a day the red and yellow

leaves made crazy patterns like that yellow,
red and green linguine we hungry children
hung to dry above the river
in a whirling, smoke-filled kitchen;
the lights of passing barges glinting off the dead,
flat, cold and bottomless water, insatiable

for everything that one time seemed insatiable;
and eventually the skin will yellow
and the nerves below the knees feel dead,
and we are again children,
huddled in the kitchen,
shades pulled against the river

as a low, late sun tints the kitchen chrome and yellow;
slanting off the river, crying that the dead
are all insatiable; and that there are no children.

Death Watch

A cat in a Rhode Island nursing center senses when
patients are about to die, and curls beside them to
mount a death-vigil in the final hours.
— *New York Times*

There was a time I fantasized a kind of geezer
in a cape and cowl, and we'd play doleful chess
in black and white, or roll the dice from leather cups;
or someone philosophical and Levantine,
who lays a finger near his eye, and smiles and shrugs.
A woman from Japan was yet another thought;
chalk-skinned and mute, inscrutable, the way they are.
Presence seemed to count, as well as metaphor.

But lately life has narrowed. What I crave
is one who'll come to smooth the sheets or wrap
me warmly, croon a little song, and help
the parts and pieces that are here behave
as now I lay me down to what shall be.
I like it when you lie so close to me.

photo by Valori Herzlich

Michael Cantor's work has appeared in *Measure, The Dark Horse, The Raintown Review, Umbrella, SCR, Margie, Chimaera* and numerous other journals, e-zines and anthologies. His honors include the New England Poetry Club Erika Mumford (2006) and Gretchen Warren (2008) Prizes. He has been a finalist or semifinalist in the Howard Nemerov, Donald Justice, Richard Wilbur and Morton Marr Award competitions. A chapbook, *The Performer,* was published by Pudding House Press in 2007. A native New Yorker, he has lived and worked in Japan, Europe and Latin America, and now lives on Plum Island, MA.

CPSIA information can be obtained at www.ICGtesting.com
Printed in the USA
BVOW071906030412

286793BV00001B/14/P